D1004999

the Gift of
Belonging

FINDING THE BACK ROADS HOME

Bradley Jon Gustafson

Palmetto Publishing Group
Charleston, SC
The Gift of Belonging
Copyright © 2020 by Bradley Jon Gustafson
All rights reserved

First Edition

Printed in the United States

ISBN-13: 978-1-7349498-0-3
ISBN-10: 1-7349498-0-5

Cover Art: "Harold Wilson's Truck" by Marlene Bulas

To Sally

CONTENTS

An Early Start   1

The Back Roads Home — Mile Markers 1–52   13

Home Free: The Gift Of The Extra Mile   107

About the Author   113

AN EARLY START

Allegiances

It is time for all the heroes to go home
if they have any, time for all of us common ones to
locate ourselves by the real things we live by.
Far to the north, or indeed in any direction,
strange mountains and creatures have always lurked-
elves, goblins, trolls, and spiders:-we
encounter them in dread and wonder,
But once we have tasted far streams, touched the gold,
found some limit beyond the waterfall,
a season changes, and we come back, changed but safe,
quiet, grateful.
Suppose an insane wind holds all the hills
while strange beliefs whine at the traveler's ears, we
ordinary beings can cling to the earth and love where
we are, sturdy for common things.

—William Stafford

William Stafford, "Allegiances" from The Way It Is: New and Selected Poems.
Copyright © 1970 by William Stafford. Reprinted with the permission of The Permission

By any world measure, mine was such a small and unremarkable gift. I found a small black-and-white photograph in one of her closet cardboard shoeboxes, pausing only momentarily before slipping the American Gothic image surreptitiously into my pocket. It took me a week to get the photo enlarged and another to find someone to write out the short Tennyson poem in calligraphy. A clerk at a framing shop near the university matted the poem and the photo separately within the bounds of one dark burgundy frame. Then late one September afternoon, Dad and I drove over to her rented town duplex apartment to give the picture back to her—her broken heart as I saw it—blown up, framed and named, and neatly wrapped in butcher's paper.

Born in 1895, my great-aunt Ollie was ninety-two and failing that brown autumn afternoon, with only a mile or two to go, six months or so, before the big sleep would finally draw her away. As Dad parked the pickup beneath the shade of the dying elm trees, I cradled the gift in my lap. He walked behind me up the concrete steps of her stoop, where her smile pushed open the screen door to welcome us.

The photograph had been taken sometime in the 1940s, and it shows Ollie standing next to two harnessed and weary mules named Jake and Pete. She smiles into the camera, her body momentarily motionless below the barn's distant, elevated haymow door. Above and just behind her, atop a grain wagon's sideboard, sits her beloved husband, Eric, who hunches slightly forward as he fails to muster a smile. He is obviously fatigued from a long day in the fields, his overalls and leather gloves dusty, his face weathered in the sun.

My single thought as I hand Ollie the package and invite her to sit down with us on her sofa is this: that nestled at the heart of love lie not common sentiments but common wounds. In the periodic depressions of our own thirties, we are rarely privy yet to our own wounded contours. Yet somehow I had always been aware of hers, my fledgling farm boy's soul having been nourished beneath the canopy of her grief, and her quiet, undying faith.

If it is true that sometimes a cigar is just a cigar, without any deeper meaning hidden within its wafting aromatic smoke, it is also true that sometimes a story is just a story. That is true, at least, until the stories we hear of others' lives begin to intersect with our own. That's when our internal empathetic sparks begin to fly. That's when deeper connective threads become visible. That's when any story becomes more than just a story.

The story of what my great-aunt Ollie and I gave to one another is just a story, of course, going back more than half a century now. But as with each story in this book, once shared it becomes more than just a story told. In a mysterious life-giving way, each of our stories when told becomes woven into the fabric of *our* story—the story of us.

This book is full of little stories about struggling to receive and give the gift of belonging, but each one is shared with a big purpose.

It is to help readers connect the dots of what it has already taken to both give and receive that gift of belonging in their own lives, not just in mine, and to encourage one another to keep connecting those dots.

The story of Ollie and Eric and me, along with all the other stories in this book, are really just simple tales about the value of bringing our honest selves to the table, whether or not we think we have anything to give to the world around us. It is a reminder that the only way to begin giving (or to begin giving again) is to start with the immeasureable gift of who we are, where we are, and what we have—not with who we wish we were, where we wish we were, or what we wish we had. It is a reminder that bringing our true and honest selves fully to life and to one another can make all the difference in the world.

As for the teller of these particular stories, it has been said that there are two kinds of Swedes: Happy Swedes and Dark Swedes. Members of my own family who have known me in my brooding hours would vouch for my being definitely of the congenital Dark Swede variety, and they're not talking about my younger brown hair and hazel eyes. I have learned how to periodically make people smile, only because I know what makes them sad.

———

In the 1950s, awash and adrift in an undulating sea of Nebraska grain, my nuclear family of five survived and thrived on a well-stocked island of chicken coops and granaries. Our barn was always busy with hay and milk, our own gardened pantry stacked high with the staples of love.

Yet my first memories are not of our island but of hers, that enchanted acre of mournful mirth half a mile away, where, for almost four decades together, Eric and Ollie harvested corn, milked cows, fed dogs, raised vegetables, butchered chickens, percolated coffee, and entertained wandering relatives. It was, we all remembered, to their island that I instinctively walked as a five-year-old the day our gentle and all-knowing Dalmatian, Duke, died, treading as I did across the divide of a stubble-strewn cornfield as across the universal threshold of loss. By the time my trembling frame reached their mailbox, my nascent soul was crying openly into the sky, searching for the solace of ears that hear.

Why does the boy remember with love and gratitude, all these decades later, the simple sight of Ollie lifting her eyes above the sill of the washhouse window, and Eric's simple act of asking the grieving boy, "What's the matter?" as he gently slid his thin frame out from beneath a grain truck in their graveled yard? Is it remembered because that was all the boy needed in his dark and dreary hour?

Isn't it remembered because that is all anyone needs in such an hour— someone to simply hear and see? Is that not why my suddenly evaporating innocence sought the cover of mercy where it could most readily be found—in the furrows of faces already chiseled by the merciless blades of grief? And as anyone could see, grief of biblical proportions lay buried deep in both of their faces.

By any world measure, the death of their boy had been such a small and unremarkable death. He had not lived long enough to be given even a name. His small stone in the hilltop graveyard above my Nebraska hometown reads simply, "A Son," along with the date on which he was stillborn in the year of our Lord, 1928. Thirty-three years old when she suffered this fateful pregnancy, Ollie had been told by the doctor, in the depths of her labor, that this would be her only child. A minister visited, neighbors brought meals, and a short religious service was hastily arranged in the churchyard four miles away with a silent vigil of family standing near. Then the death became nothing but one more tragic miscarriage of hope swept beneath the carpet of time.

Years later, Ollie gave me an old valise suitcase stored for decades in her attic, containing the uniform Eric had worn in the trenches of France, complete with gas mask, leggings, and a captured lighter with *GOTT MIT UNS* engraved on its side. Fighting with General Jack Pershing's American Expeditionary Force in the last months of 1918, Eric had been gassed by a mustard cloud and left for dead in a muddy field.

He lay for hours until a horse-drawn cart of a death detail passed by a second time. Some unnamed soldier saw him take a breath and said, "Oh, what the hell," and threw him on just in case he would pull through. An older relative told me once that war had softened Eric in all the right ways. He was a man who had seen the river of life and death overflowing the war-strewn banks of the world, and part of it had become lodged there where anyone could see it, in his sad, rural Nebraska eyes.

And so it was after the war and after the stillbirth that my great-uncle Eric and great-aunt Ollie settled into their life together without children, without the hope of family, yet surrounded by siblings and neighbors, mules and barns, and relatives.

No one had more community-wide birthday parties at their home than Eric and Ollie did; no one served more coffee at later hours. Driving home through the darkened landscape, returning home from church or a late-night check of the fields, my father would always look out across the fields for their yard light. The rule was if the light was on, so was the coffee, and we would always stop.

I still think these many years later, rightly or wrongly, that I was the most special among all her young relations to her—perhaps the greatest tribute to her adoptive skills. The role she came throughout her life to play for me was no less than that of a full-fledged grandmother, even long after that cold day in 1960 when Eric's war-wounded lungs and heart finally gave out in spite of forty years of fresh air, and he slumped over in the yard one fall afternoon during corn-picking season and died, with Ollie and dinner waiting on him in the house.

What I remember now are the little things that were huge when I was a boy. Like being asked by Ollie to mow her yard and always being welcome in her refrigerator. She and I played circus in her barn, with horse blankets draped over sawhorses to look like bears. She let me swim in her livestock tank and sat beside me as I drove her car down three country miles as far as the church. I can still smell, with remarkable acuity, both her incomparable afternoon cinnamon rolls and the dusty jackets of the two devotionals she read from each morning before she left the breakfast table. When, on occasion, she tucked me in for the night in my own bedroom upstairs in her cold and drafty attic, I fell into an eternal reverie with the rhythms of her antique clock, as it ticked away the hours and the years.

———

There was clearly a mysterious river of mercy that sustained Ollie on her own back road home; hers was decidedly a back road if you count unexpected grief and unplanned fateful detours as a back way rather than the straight way to the soul's salvation and to that life full of connection we all envision when we're young. As for me, when I was born two generations later, Ollie's personal depths were anchored deep in the channels of that river, as she guided my own immersion in the same waters flowing downriver for me. Ollie was a woman of the twentieth century who had nothing and yet was able to give everything, by simply being present as she was to all who surrounded her. She was elderly and poor, and she lived isolated, a mile from the river and twelve flatland miles from town. She was uneducated, childless, wounded, and widowed, and she made all the difference in the world.

———————

And so it was a short six months before she was to die, with her broken heart still beating with that peculiar love that has been drenched in tears, that I decided to give Ollie my gift. I wanted her to see what I could see. In my own early thirties by this time, unmarried and child-less with not much sense of my own future, I found myself with this acute sensibility concerning her past—a past that I now knew was an interwoven thread in the fabric of my own.

She opened the package, but began to cry and could not read the poem. She handed it to my father, who after a moment passed it to me. It was Tennyson's *As Thro' the Land At Eve We Went*, and I read it for all of us, aloud.

> *As thro' the land at eve we went, And pluck'd the ripen'd ears, We fell out, my wife and I,*
> *O we fell out I know not why, And kiss'd again with tears.*
>
> *And blessings on the falling out That all the more endears,*
> *When we fall out with those we love And kiss again with tears!*
>
> *For when we came, where lies the child We lost in other years,*
> *There above the little grave, O there above the little grave,*
> *We kiss'd again with tears.*

By the time the poem was finished, Ollie was weeping; my dad was weeping; I was weeping. Yet rarely, if ever, have I been in a room filled with more genuine joy. It was the shared joy of being known and seen, the joy of being connected by love to the world, the joy of a grief observed and acknowledged and somehow, miraculously, redeemed.

I do not remember so much my Aunt Ollie's tears that day. What I will never forget is the joy with which she suddenly leapt up and ran to her front stoop, pushing open the storm door and yelling for her neighbor across the street to come. Her neighbor was working in his yard, old Mr. Higby; tall and soft-spoken, he was the retired town funeral director. "Come and see!" she hollered to him.

"What is it?" I heard quiet Mr. Higby ask, the man who had buried Eric thirty years before, and so many others of her loved ones. He leaned his rake against the brick wall of his home. "What is it?" he asked softly again.

All she could muster as she stood on the threshold, waiting for him to come, was "Oh, come see!"

Tell all the truth but tell it slant—

Tell all the truth but tell it slant— Success in Circuit lies
Too bright for our infirm Delight The Truth's superb surprise

As Lightning to the Children eased With explanation kind
The Truth must dazzle gradually
Or every man be blind

—Emily Dickinson

A WORD ABOUT THE
GIVING OF GIFTS

When it comes to pouring our gifts into the rich swirl of community, we bring what we have to give and nothing more. But the aim of giving is always, at its best, toward what others need rather than toward what we need—and knowing the difference between the two can make a big difference.

I sat in Mike's pickup, ready to leave for the airport, after a week together in the Northwest with "the Birds." He is my best friend of forty years or more, and I trust the aim of every supportive comment or critique he sends my way—the latter of which isn't often, as he is so very, very generous with his belief.

Mike and I had in a former lifetime once stood quickened, twenty feet from a grizzly bear and her two cubs in a Canadian national park. "You know how it is in the woods," he started, "when a bear goes after a honeycomb in an empty stump or a hollow tree?"

Well, yeah, I said.

He continued, "You know how the bear swats away at all the bees who are guarding the honey, swatting away at its own face and ears, keeping the swarming bees at bay, but keeping on because it wants the honey?"

Yeah, I see it, I said.

"Well, my friend," he said calmly, "that's how I am with your words."

I smiled, as I am wont to do, but I felt the sting common to every writer. How does one make honey without a lot of bees?

"I love your words," he said, "but just remember, we're not after the bees; we're after the honey."

LOOKING BACK TO FIND
OUR WAY FORWARD

A year or two ago, thirty years or so after Ollie left the earth, my 94-year-old mother and I took a slow, leisurely drive through the square-mile sections of countryside where she and Dad had made a home for us so many decades ago. Mom and I each wanted to see some of the sights of bygone years. We drove by the pond south of the barn where we used to fish and ice-skate, the old schoolhouse on the corner, the barn at Ollie's place where she had played circus with me as a boy, the farmhouse of an uncle and an aunt where as children we would be dismissed after an evening meal to go play upstairs, but where we kids would instead open the heating vents cut through the upstairs floorboards so we could listen to the adults still talking around the dinner table below. Then we passed the wooded ravine where I shot my first pheasant while hunting with Cocoa, and we even drove down to see the old tabernacle and cabins of Polk Bible Camp. We saw all these sites vividly as we passed by, even though they weren't there.

They were all cornfields now.

I told Mom our drive was making me sad, as I didn't seem able to see anything of what was in front of me; I could see only what used to be. The pleasures of pure nostalgia can sometimes turn into an absence of hope in the future, meaning that if we start thinking the best of life is in our past, we've ceased believing that the best is yet to be.

But nostalgia is also a way for me of remembering once again the road I traveled as I strove to find my way into a place of true belonging. I suspect mine isn't the only journey home that has felt more like a back road than a front road, in its rolling pastoral contours, its ruts and ragged detours.

But something else is visible in those cornfields now: that mysterious grace that had passed through those times along with all the life. One need not be religious to see mercy in one's memories. I saw clearly now that my back road home had been a river road too—never far from that same river of grace that Ollie had so vulnerably come to depend upon, and know so well.

3

NO ONE'S LIFE OR WORK IS TOO SMALL TO BE PART OF THE WHOLE

We build trust by giving trust. On a bright sunny day in the late fifties, my father taught me one early July how to drive, at the age of five. In my red shorts and bare feet, I was riding next to him in the front seat of a 1941 black Ford pickup, its rear bed full of irrigation tubes. My dad pulled onto a dusty field road along a freshly dug irrigation ditch and stopped. "I want you to stand over here," he said, and I slid over and stood upright on the driver's seat, placing my little hands on the big steering wheel. Dad stood outside the open cab door and placed his left hand on the clutch pedal, placed a short two-by-four between the seat and the accelerator, and put the truck in gear. "Brad," he said to me, "I want you to look at that well down there and don't take your eyes off it, OK?" I nodded. He then let out the clutch and I was off. He jumped into the back of the pickup and started throwing irrigation tubes into the dry rows as we passed by. It was only a quarter mile stretch on a small farm in a remote corner of the world, but it was nothing less than a coast-to-coast drive to me. I disobeyed my father only once, to look back. Halfway to the well I turned, curious for an instant, to glance back through the rear window of the cab. I was stunned to discover that my dad wasn't watching me.

He was working on the task that had been given to him, and simply presumed that I was doing the same. I turned and kept driving, my hands locked and my feet firm, standing ever so slightly taller than when I had first started out.

NO PLACE IS TOO REMOTE TO
BE PART OF THE WHOLE

One acre of land can be, in the heart of a child, the center of the entire universe. I don't remember isolation; I remember belonging to something larger than myself. In kindergarten, first grade, and second grade, I remember *being* the kindergarten, first grade, and second grade. Academically, for the last time in my life, I had no peers. But I did my lessons with Lois, who *was* the grade ahead of me. As we sat at our little desks with the empty little two-inch-round ink holes cut into the surface wood near the top where the pencil grooves were lathed in, and as we cut out pictures of a goat with our little scissors and pasted them with goopy glue beside the word *goat* on the opposite page, together we watched and listened as our older sisters and cousins in fifth and sixth grades did long division on the blackboard in front of the classroom with Miss Schack, our common teacher.

We never let our grades get in the way of our education. Nine grades in one room, and I don't remember it ever being chaotic. Miss Schack may beg to differ. It wasn't chaotic or unordered; it was exciting. There were two "seniors" during my last year there, as eighth grade was as far as the school could take you: my cousin Roylene, who lived east across the cornfield, and Kathy, who lived a mile and a half north near the river and rode her horse to school and let it graze in the ditch all day. Miss Schack gave me sixty words a week to memorize and define, and gave me the test on Friday just before recess, with recess the reward for passing. I was six years old in an extended family of tee-totalers when I learned to define the word *keg*.

5

TOGETHER IS AS TOGETHER DOES

Community, no matter how small by world standards, can be vulnerable and exhilarating at the same time. What is education, anyway, other than an exposure to something you don't know, and a community connection to people with whom you are not familiar? I imagine it was some kind of heating oil tank that stood on iron stilts on the north side of the schoolhouse—the only side without windows or a door. There was one stove that served to heat us, and our food, too, on occasion. Fifteen minutes before the noon recess, Miss Schack would announce the hour and encourage anyone with cheese sandwiches or soup in their lunch pails to fetch them from the coatroom and bring them in to place on the hot stove. By noon the cheese sandwiches would be *grilled* cheese sandwiches. My lunch pail had sailboats and motorboats on it, and it had a soup thermos inside with a cap that served as a cup. At noon recess, after we all ate, we were sent out to play together at whatever came to us: games of pom-pom- pullaway were most common, or basketball at the two wooden, double-post backboards that had nothing but dirt and grass beneath and between them.

One winter in a blizzard, Miss Schack knew she couldn't send us out to play, but she also knew she was going to have a full afternoon of it if we didn't burn off a little energy. So she gave us our orders: After you visit the outhouses, boys to the left, girls to the right, everyone has to run around the schoolhouse five times, touching the walls all the way around, before you can come back in. I could barely see the walls, but I could also barely contain the fun we were all having in the storm, together.

6

TRUE COMMUNITY OUTLIVES
AND OUTLASTS ITSELF

The value of charity for all with which we build our institutions will outlast, and outlive, the institutions themselves for which that charity has been built. How long did it take others to build what we have taken for granted our whole life long? My father attended the same one-room schoolhouse as I did, as did my great-aunt Ollie and her seven siblings only sixty years earlier. When Ollie was six years old, her father, who had helped build the school, sent her and her siblings off down the lane in a drizzling rain to school early one day in 1901, as their mother was in labor with her eighth living child (five had died in childbirth). Ollie's father had run a tavern in Chicago after emigrating from Sweden just after the Civil War—before getting saved at a big Chicago tent revival meeting and migrating to Nebraska farm country "out west." He walked to the end of their lane that day to catch the mailman's horse and wagon, get his copy of the *Tribune*, and glean any breaking news from the driver that might not yet have made the week-old Chicago paper. The mailman shouted as soon as he saw my great-grandfather, "President McKinley's been shot; Teddy Roosevelt is our new president!"

Andrew Gustaf Gustafson took the heartbreaking news of his new country to heart as best he could and announced, "Well, we've just had a baby boy, and we didn't know what to name him. But that settles it: we'll name him Theodore McKinley!"

Ollie loved her little brother Teddy all his life, although he was considered a bit of a black sheep in a pretty pure extended religious flock by the time he died in Hollywood sixty-three years later. But he had attended the same schoolhouse for nine years himself, and never, ever had any sense that he wasn't fully a child of the community whenever he did come back to visit. He was right. District 59 had closed and the building sold and moved off two years earlier by the time Teddy's body was brought back from California to be buried in the local Nebraska churchyard. His long back road ended where it had begun: at home.

7

TO BELONG IS ITS OWN REWARD

Community does not eliminate, but rather illuminates, the uniqueness of the individuals who make it up. I learned from the second dog I ever loved that running wild doesn't have to mean trouble—which is what any young boy can learn from dogs who run free. By the time I was seven, Cocoa was our maturing English springer spaniel, a dog who was gentle with kids and other people but fierce and no-nonsense in a dogfight. And to boot, he ran in a gang. All seven or eight dogs in this gang slept at their own farms at night but roamed together during the day, returning again to their own proprietary food bowls near suppertime. On hot summer days we'd surprise these loose- running outlaws as they were cooling off together in a ditch miles from home, up to their necks in brome grass and muddy from head to tail after frolicking in some neighbor's irrigation ditches. A black Lab, an immigrant Weimaraner Ollie's brother Ted had sent her from California, an Irish setter, an Alaskan husky, a collie destined to die in a mowing accident, an indecipherable mix, another sweet nondescript mutt, and a working dog named Rex are the ones I remember.

They were all working dogs, of course, if you count the work of bringing joy to the land and people who surrounded them. The dogs were at once easy to feed and hard to displease. They had their own concerns and their own pursuits, largely independent of any single farm's economic welfare. Status meant very little to them, but not nothing. They had their own intra-community dynamics. They all respected each other as equals when they dug dirt or stared down raccoons or barked at badger holes together. But each looked up with great envy at Kip-Nik, the Alaskan husky who rode in a car to town on Friday nights to serve as our school's athletic mascot. The dogs were in awe of Kip, but not just for his privileged presence on such a prominent public platform. They remained in awe because for all their incessant individual talk, they each knew he was the only one among them who had ever actually *caught* a jack rabbit.

8

AN ADULT COMMUNITY'S POVERTY IS A CHILD'S WEALTH

The charity of community hospitality matters, and an abundance of money has very little to do with it. I always thought of my parents as rich, as when I was a little boy what did I know about wealth? Mom raised a whole brooder house full of chickens, collected an abundance of eggs, and separated pails full of cream from our cows. As a boy, Dad had hunted for food in our south woods for his parents' table, had picked corn by hand, and had grown to manage land for others. There was nothing they couldn't do. To his dying day, Dad knew exactly how much money he had in the bank, despite some late-onset dementia. The luxury of eating out once a week had come fifteen years into their marriage, and even decades later, when Dad insisted on picking up the dinner tab for fifteen to twenty people, I'd catch him slipping his finger into the coin return on the pay phone on his way out to the Cadillac, just in case there might be a dime in there.

One day when I was small, he unbolted a hand-crank drill press from his garage workbench, drove over to put it in a neighbor's farm sale, got a full seven dollars for it, and drove to town to get the money in the bank to avoid an overdraft. As a six-year-old boy, I never knew of course; bank money meant nothing to me. At the end of our one-room schoolhouse year, all I remember is our families coming together for a big picnic of abundance in the schoolhouse yard. Before we all went across the road into the Bergmark pasture to gather up dried cow pies to use as softball bases, we wallowed together in our riches, eating home-raised fried chicken, fruit salad, and mashed potato casserole, and we chose for dessert between big pieces of chocolate frosting cake and tall slices of my mom's rhubarb meringue pie.

9

RELIGIOUS PRACTICE MAKES US KNOW WE'RE IMPERFECT

At its best, religion aims our hearts toward a larger belonging, rather than toward itself as the ultimate goal. The schoolhouse on the corner as one crossroad of early youth; the rural white clapboard church three miles away as a second. As kids, we took baths once a week on Saturday nights whether we needed them or not, but we attended church at least three times a week and sometimes four, whether we wanted to go or not: Sunday morning school for teaching and then church for worship, Sunday evening for more singing and another sermon, and then Wednesday night prayer meeting. Thursday nights, too, if a missionary family was in town with slides and maybe snakeskins from Africa to show. There were two weeks of vacation Bible school in the summer, and then at least one week at our Bible camp twenty-five miles away, built over many years next to a creek that often flooded the cabins, most of which were named for places in the Scriptures.

Family Camp Sunday brought in relatives and friends from around the state, and many generational families were born there romantically beneath the elm trees and the roof of the open-air tabernacle, with crickets chirping along as steady percussion to the hymns and the preaching. Hand-hewn wooden benches stood anchored by their own weight on a concrete floor, with tree branches and fireflies where walls could be but weren't. The candy canteen didn't open until after the last song was over, but its Pixy Stix, Popsicles, and Root Beer Barrels were dancing in our heads the whole time, waiting patiently for us down the hill in the dark afterward beneath the canteen's yellow, bug-less light bulbs. Something even sweeter than hard candy was supposed to get into the children's hearts during those long hours of restless homesickness in the pews, and it undoubtedly did. All we knew at the time, however, was that we were so very, very happy when finally, we were let out.

10

BORDERS ARE TO CROSS
AND GROW BY

The message of belonging is dangerous, as no one can say definitively just where to draw the line. As they say, where you stumble, there lies your treasure. I think that's how it goes. Or maybe it is where your treasure lies, there you can expect to stumble. The religious message of belonging in the world is what has always tripped me up; I've taken it literally as a true believer. I remember riding as a late teen in the backseat of my parents' car down a gravel road one night on the way back from church in the country, trying to fall asleep against the window and the dark. I could almost take you there to the exact place seven miles from town, where trees grow along a creek to the east but not to the west. I decided in that moment to attend a church-related college two thousand miles away in a foreign country, if you count Canada as foreign. It turned out to be a religiously sanctioned way to run away from home for a few years after high school.

My parents had taken my brother and me to British Columbia to visit the campus of a church-related school after a summer church conference trip to Seattle the year before, and I was enchanted not only with the college's geographical terrain but with its promise of sheer *difference*. I knew the world I knew, but I also knew deep down that it wasn't the *only* world out there to which I belonged. I went with my parents' blessing but, as it turned out later, not exactly with their approval. Once I went into the larger world, it turned out I could never quite fully come back.

M. Scott Peck, the author of *The Road Less Traveled*, wrote once of attending his thirtieth high school reunion. He sat in the bleachers at a football game; the smells were the same, and some of the faces were even the same. But he had been away, and he could never be completely at home again where home had been. He likened it biblically to never again having any place to lay his head.

HOME IS ALWAYS WHERE
THE HEART ONCE WAS

One of the benefits of leaving home is that it's only from away that one can come home again—and there, "at the end of all our exploring," as T.S. Eliot wrote, "arrive where we started and know the place for the first time." I lived in Vancouver off and on for eight years in my twenties, and then came home to Nebraska when my Canadian exploring was at its end. I've lived in Colorado, California, South Carolina, and New Jersey for years at a time since then, but I inevitably find myself back on home turf: sitting in familiar coffee shops on Nebraska's familiar crossroads, taking in the familiar conversations of familiar people, walking on rural gravel as though it were the touchstone of all of life's precious metals the world over.

Garrison Keillor left Minnesota to live in New York City, later lived in Denmark, and finally returned to St. Paul. "If I'm not from here," he said, "I'm not from anywhere."

12

A SEE-THROUGH FENCE IS BETTER THAN AN OPAQUE WALL

Artificial, temporary limits on belonging can serve, but only to get us into the real game. In my well-regulated rural religious community, the fences around the moral offenses were well defined. Just to list a few: no movies, no drinking, no swearing, no smoking, no face cards, no pool halls, no drugs, no premarital sex (it might lead to dancing), and no sleeping in on Sunday mornings. I attended a church-related junior college two thousand miles away from home, accompanied by more than a few family friends and cousins from my own people. That made this college risk safe enough. The crisis turned out to come from the college attendees from elsewhere who shared my faith but not my fences. Once a fence is seen through and maybe walked through and lightning doesn't strike, it's very hard to believe in the fence anymore, even if you still fear the offense that gave rise to it. I grew my hair long and started walking (and talking) my way through fences.

In her later years, my mother herself began walking Friday nights to the corner movie house with church friends; fought her insomnia by playing solitaire on the computer alone at night; sipped a glass of wine one evening with some friends across the hall at her independent living home; admitted that one regret she had in life was that she had never learned to dance; and, to top it all off, asked once when I came to visit if I would take her to the bank to deposit a plastic cup full of nickels, to launder her winnings from a weekly bingo game. The external moral plumb line from my cherished early childhood was swaying in the breeze, but I let it swing without judgment. I realized my mother was simply leaving home and going to college with me in Canada, forty years later, at long last.

DISORIENTATION CAN BE A MILE MARKER ON THE ROAD TO TRUE BELONGING

Every single moment of truth along the road helps lead to all the rest. If we're seeking truth, I've found that the truth itself will speak up in unexpected moments. Having come home in my late twenties to Nebraska after being away, I remember a sense of grounded lostness— grounded in the familiar and in the strange at the same time. One cool night in the summer of my return, I found myself riding through the country with Paul, a former classmate. Paul had spent his years away on a Navy carrier as a helicopter hydraulics mechanic. If I had been the class goody-two-shoes, he had been our badass. He came from a broken home in California, smoked and drank and laughed at all the wrong times and places, and he fought both with his hands and with his stare. We were in a cherry red 1931 Model A 5-Window Coupe he had restored himself from scratch, and we pulled up beneath the stars on a gravel road six miles from town, just shy of a stopped freight train. He turned off the car as we stepped outside, and with Michelobs in our hands, we put pennies on the tracks. We were the last people in high school anyone would ever have thought could become friends. But I had changed, and so had he. Paul was a man of few words but deep feeling.

"You know what life is like?" he asked after a long silence under the moon, as the train cars began suddenly jerking to life.

I said no, tell me.

He said, "It's like you're suspended in space and there's all this chaos and crazy stuff floating around you, but you're OK because you've got hold of this rope. And then one day, you're just hanging out and suddenly you see the other end of your rope go floating past."

I took one last sip and a deep breath, as I felt in that moment, strangely, just a little less lost.

14

PASSION IS AS PASSION DOES

Working with strangers out in the world can be its own reward; you get to know many strangers, including yourself. In my Canada years I got caught in the vocational trap of searching for my one true passion, as if it just lay there somewhere like a golden ticket in the weeds, waiting to be discovered if I didn't get distracted by things beneath me. "Follow your bliss" was kind of a seventies thing. When I would say from time to time that I was finding myself, my dad's refrain was inevitably "Get a job; you'll show up." What he didn't tell me was how long it might take. But I did decide to leave my one true special and elusive passion where it lay for a while, and at least show up at work.

To the question "What do you want to do with your life?" I changed my answer from "I don't know yet" to "I don't know; what have you got?" There was nothing in my twenties or thirties that could be discerned as a true professional path, but for my soul the path was true. I discovered that even a ditch can be a road if you keep moving.

I worked some construction as well as on family farms, wrote about water resources for the university ag college, spent three years in Denver working food and beverage for Hyatt by day and as a UPS clerk by night, and spent seven years paying the rent (and psychiatrist bills) in Charleston, giving historic tours of the city. My dad was right about one thing: I got a lot of jobs and the world showed up—the world as it really is. Somewhere in the middle of it all, I started showing up too, and then Sally showed up, and then a professional possibility showed up. I guess that's what it means when they say 90 percent of success at life is showing up.

15

SUFFERING DOES NOT COME WITH EXPLANATIONS

Personal suffering is inescapably part of the landscape we travel through, and when a heart breaks early, there's little to be done but to let our own hearts break with it. My cousin Rick had awakened me early our first morning together with a start. We were both five years old, sharing an upstairs double bed in the south room of my parents' farmhouse. He had just returned from Africa with his missionary parents, and it was the beginning of a beautiful friendship. Outside it was dark at that early hour, all the bedrooms in the house being full but still silent, and he whispered to me, "Let's go."

I followed him out of our assigned quarters as we slid on our jeans and shirts and tiptoed down the wooden stairs to the kitchen. There Rick and I rifled through my mom's cupboards and the fridge until we found two bowls, spoons, a carton of milk, and a box of Life cereal. We sat for just a few hallowed minutes alone in the dark, across from one another at the kitchen table, listening only to each other eat, with not one authoritative creature stirring in all the house.

We kept waking up one another's souls many times in the years that followed. I thought he was smarter; he thought I was. I thought he was endangering his life with his rebellious lifestyle; he thought I was endangering my soul in my over-restraint. He told me once when I was stuck in my thinking that I needed to think with my feet. He thought I stayed in things too long; I thought he didn't stay in things long enough. I never knew where his pain came from, but he told me over coffee many years later exactly when it became too much. He was sitting on a family sofa, a twelve-year-old boy alone in his family home late one afternoon in the suburbs of Chicago, and decided he wasn't going to feel the pain anymore. Two years later, a fellow student in the school lot offered him a little white pill, and it proved over time to have marked, at such a young age, the beginning of the end.

16

THOSE WHO WILL RECEIVE NO HELP WILL SOON HAVE NO HELP TO GIVE

Naming the door can be the key to opening it. The end of the great friendship of my youth came with an evening phone call in my mid-thirties. My cousin Rick called one night and we talked for two hours, about elusive girls and unfinished PhD studies, authoritative parents, annoying younger brothers and other fun things. I realized only later that he was calling to say goodbye. When they found his body in a motel room in Mobile three days later, dead from an intentional overdose, the writing was on the wall for my own life too. I did not share his drug and alcohol addictions, but I did share with him his stuck-ness, and I knew that life as I was living it was over too.

That crisis became my beginning. A month and a half later, I sat one afternoon a thousand miles away in Charleston, pouring out my aching, conflicted soul to a friend. My friend is a great listener, so much so that she interrupted me in the depths of my angst and said, "I'm not your therapist." Then she held out a piece of paper between her fingers and said, "But I have a number."

I was with a brilliant, somewhat eccentric psychiatrist for seven years in twice-weekly groups and a few dinner parties—I would describe him as a ponytailed combination of Sigmund Freud and Zorba the Greek—and he eventually became a friend and a mentor. He did not fix me or change anything about me. But his presence of mind and heart and humor, as he welcomed us every week up crooked stairs into his upper-room study, gave me the space I needed to heal, to get my feet on the ground, to start moving again. He used to say, "Yesterday's solutions are today's problems." He taught me well that it wasn't my problems but my solutions that were constricting my life. Or as Will Rogers would have it, it wasn't what I didn't know that had gotten me in trouble; it was what I knew for absolute sure that just wasn't so. Talk therapy isn't a cure for everything by a long shot, but without freedom of speech, it can be hard for anyone to learn to breathe deeply on one's own.

BELONGING IS EVEN
BIGGER THAN DEATH

Death is always a community life event. It was a packed church house that gathered for Rick's funeral, having heard John Donne's bell toll for us all. It turned out to be indeed true that no matter how lonely at one's end, "No man is an island, entire of itself; every man is a piece of the continent, a part of the main ... any man's death diminishes me," though it falls into the sea. And yet, truth be told, Rick never awakened me in life to the same degree he did in his death. As I stood to say a word at his service, I found myself in tears, blowing my nose into a microphone and a borrowed handkerchief, saying only that throughout our mutual years of trouble, I had discovered there to be no possible way to help lift a friend into a larger life, apart from just trying to keep walking into that larger life myself.

Every step I have taken since then, I have inevitably taken with Rick as a backdrop to the picture; with every personal story that unfolds, I can still imagine telling him later that night over some late coffee at a Village Inn pancake house twenty miles between our respective homes, each of us much older now, my hearing him laugh or maybe cry, or my simply observing him mournfully gazing out the window through his beautifully heartbroken eyes. Every step I have taken without him since his death, in marriage and in profession, in spirit and in imagination, strangely does not seem to have taken me farther away from him, but closer.

In the thirty years since, our common rural Nebraska community has buried his father and then my father, and then my own brother as well. But John Donne's continent of life itself has not crumbled, even though these loved ones have fallen into the sea. I no longer grieve the years we weren't given. I celebrate now and remember with gratitude the ones we were.

18

IT IS STRANGERS WHO OPEN THE EYES OF OTHER STRANGERS' SOULS

It's not always our eyes that don't quite see straight; it's our souls.

She had introduced me to the seashell-laden barrier island beaches of South Carolina. Now I was introducing her to the cornhusk-strewn autumn banks of Nebraska's rivers. We had so much in common that I thought she might be the one. I drove her in my dad's pickup down a gravel county road, an eighth of a mile from the tree line to our left, having just watched together thousands of snow geese lifting off at a river preserve north of Omaha.

"Oh, look at the goose blind," I said casually, pointing through the trees across a narrow field.

"Where?" Sally asked. "Over there, see it?"

"No, where?"

I did a U-turn in the road and drove back, more slowly. There.

"What is it, a goose blind?" she asked. We turned again. This time I stopped and rolled down my window, and she leaned across me, staring at what she did not, could not, understand.

"It's a goose blind," I said. "See, over there in those trees to the left, you can see the hunters' pickups."

The light came on. "Oh, isn't that sweet?" she said. "They made a place for the geese to hide."

I cocked my head like the RCA dog in those old Victrola ads. I knew I had heard something, but for the life of me I couldn't figure out who it was had said it. She saw grace and charity and fairness where I had only ever seen hunger and stealth and deception. I found myself ambushed by her charitable eyes, and I've been a goner ever since.

CHOOSING THE ROAD OF
MUTUALITY MEANS GIVING
UP OTHER ROADS

Accepting the challenge of loving can mean the end of life as we know it. Twenty-two years ago my wife, Sally, and I got married in our early forties, each for the first time, a little late but far from sorry. We joke that we are a couple of decades developmentally delayed. We thus have no children except each other, but we can be a handful. We had a short seven-year engagement period, during which I wrestled in therapy with some emotional resistance to growing up into my life work. Resistance to growth is human, of course, but I knew I wanted to marry Sally, and I wasn't going to let a little vocational immaturity on my part get in the way.

Sally is a clinical psychologist and can spot a Freudian slip from two rooms away. As our wedding day approached, I for some subconscious reason began referring to it as the upcoming funeral. "What if we had our funeral at 2 p.m. instead of at 4?" I would ask. You can imagine how well that went over. Then three weeks before our ceremony, my grandmother died in Minnesota, and as we drove there, I began asking what time Grandma's wedding was going to be. I felt bad about this, until Sally started doing it as well. Driving past a Nebraska cemetery on the way home, she wondered aloud what we might want on our wedding stone. Marriage for each of us was the end of life as we knew it, and we each found ourselves ready for that end, along with the new beginning to come.

WE ARE LESS ALONE IN OUR CHARITABLE ADVENTURES TOWARD ONE ANOTHER THAN WE THINK

Scarcity, like beauty, is in the eye of the beholder. Sally and I were married by a Presbyterian minister in a 320-year-old Circular church in Charleston, South Carolina—a church that had originally been called the Dissenters' Meeting Church. The building had been ruined three times by fire, war, and earthquake, and for years after the Civil War, the church building was nothing but a pile of rubble in the midst of an old graveyard. But the dissenters had kept coming. Finally, in 1895, the same old bricks were used to rebuild a fourth time, and here we were, 102 years later, getting married in its wooden interior, the church surrounded by blossoming azaleas and dogwood trees, standing witness amid the silence of weathered slate gravestones.

The day of the wedding ceremony felt so filled with joy, mixed with tears, that we had only one regret: empty seats. We regretted terribly that we hadn't invited even more family and friends, that we hadn't somehow found a way to fill all the pews. We felt badly, thinking of how many we knew who were not with us. But all regrets were dispelled when Sally's cousin told her, "It's always good to have empty seats at a wedding . . . so all the angels will have a place to sit . . . the angels, who are always in attendance at such events."

I cannot think of that wedding now without seeing the sanctuary filled to the rafters.

21

THE END IS WHERE WE
TRULY BEGIN

How much work does it take to get us to the starting line of true living? I used to drolly say, when I was deep in therapy and I thought I was lost and all my worldly prospects were behind me, that "these will one day be called my 'wilderness years.'" As I look back, I've come to believe that wilderness years are underrated. When I was deep in the forest after Rick's death, I started choosing things for myself, almost as if for the first time. I chose for myself my own city, "my woman," my therapy, my own vocational pursuit and my own sport.

After an early history of going out for every sport that was offered, sometimes more out of peer pressure than of compelling interest or ability, I chose for myself for three grueling but invigorating years, the sport of Tae Kwon Do. Sometimes in a gym, sometimes on a beach, forms and more forms, sparring and more sparring, confidence and more confidence. My local teacher, Dr. Emmel, a Fifth Dan Master and Mr. Son, the Ninth Dan Grandmaster, in combination were the real deal. Mr. Son had taught the U.S. Army before emigrating to New York City in the 1960s. He handed me a first-degree black belt one afternoon after a camp in New York and a tournament in Charleston and said in his low broken English, waving his finger at me, "Good, good, good." I felt prouder at that moment than any time I donned a football helmet back in the day. The next morning on the beach at dawn, he returned from a solo five-mile run (in his seventies by then), and he lined up all the seconds and the thirds and the fourths and the fifths for forms. He then called all the proud new firsts to listen up. We stepped forward proudly on the sand in our bleached white *gis* and freshly embroidered dark black belts.

"Back of line!" he shouted. "Back of line!"

We were once again in the starting gate, having earned the right to begin learning at a whole new level.

22

LIFE IS SO MUCH MORE THAN WHAT WE THINK ABOUT IT

Letting new life in can require letting old convictions go. In my early forties I married and then promptly left my wife for the East Coast. My new South Carolina beach bride stayed in western Nebraska while I took off to attend seminary in New Jersey. Intellectually Princeton, both the seminary I attended and the university next door, was rarefied air. I guess I was smart enough to get in, but the first thing I learned was that there are smart people in the world, and there are *really smart* people in the world. But as they say, if you're always the smartest person in the room, you're in the wrong rooms. So I just grabbed onto the academic bumper and let myself get dragged through the gravel for three years, hoping something of something would rub off.

I've also heard it said that the real sign of smartness is knowing how much you don't know; by that measure, I felt myself getting smarter and smarter every day. But the discipline was in more than opening my mind to take good notes and tests and write cogent papers without letting myself sound dumb. The real discipline of my three years there was in opening my heart to new people—some of them *really smart*—and to their own honest and hard-won perspectives that didn't always mesh with my past experience, nor with the theology I had merely inherited by sheer chance of birth and nurture. The discipline that saved me there was the discipline of eating with those I was not comfortable eating with, and listening (with my mouth full) to those I was not comfortable listening to.

Some students could be heard near graduation claiming proudly that they had made it through Princeton without Princeton getting through them. They had succeeded in leaving Princeton Theological Seminary after three years with absolutely the very same theology and perspective on the world that they had come in with. I would call that a waste of three perfectly good years of life. If you already know everything, why go to school at all?

CONVERSATION IS ALWAYS A
RADICAL ACT OF HOSPITALITY

If you can talk about the weather, you can talk to anyone. In my
first year at seminary, without my wife or a car, I lived in a dormitory
with the single students (a monk with leave privileges, I called myself).
My room was fifty feet from the cafeteria and the main lecture hall,
a hundred yards from the world-class theological library, four hundred yards from Princeton University's main campus, and two hundred
yards from an off-Broadway theater and the New Jersey Transit train
to New York. At the cafeteria, I was on the board plan, which meant I
could eat all I wanted from the fairly wide selections at any meal. It also
meant, since I had already paid, that I was inclined to eat everything
I could to make it pay. I knew (and my wife knew) that desserts could
easily become the downfall of this culinary/economic agenda. So I de-
vised an ingenious plan that I thought might also solve the issue of my
not feeling that I belonged.

I decided to take the richest dessert I could find at every meal and
take it to my table with me . . . along with four or five forks. Our cafeteria was set up with many eight- or nine-person round tables, and it
was easier for me to sit down with strangers if I was bearing the gift
of sugar with me. As I told them when I offered them forks: if you're
asked later if you bought or took dessert from the cafeteria line, you
can honestly say no. A little opening conversation about dessert with

strangers was like talking about the weather in a socially (or theologically) tense room. It's nice, and ultimately it always leads to conversation about much more than the weather.

24

LISTENING TO OUR OWN STORY ALWAYS LEADS TO THE LARGER STORY

Investing ourselves in the story of charity for all can be personally disruptive to our own story, to say the least. Poets and prophets of old sang of the hard task of "every hill and mountain being made low, rough places being made plain, crooked places being made straight." On my way alone to Brooklyn for the first time by train, through New York's Penn Station one day many years ago, I remember watching an impeccably dressed African American businessman in a three-piece suit reading the paper on a raised chair, as beneath him a middle-aged white man attentively shined his shoes. It was a searing image of some rough places slowly being made smooth.

I caught the first of three subways south and east beneath the river to Montauk Avenue, on my way to helping a French anti-poverty organization conduct what it called a Street Library: reading to children on the sidewalks in one of the poorest neighborhoods in Brooklyn, perhaps in all of America. I arrived at the wrong stop, walked for about a mile, took two bus rides, talked to two metro cops behind glass, and for two of the longest hours in my life to that point, finally learned what it was to be different. Meaning I was, for the first time in my life, a racial minority of one, for as far as my eyes could see or my feet walk. I found my fears in dire need of the very hospitality I had nobly thought I was coming to bring.

SMALL MOMENTS OF
MUTUAL RECOGNITION CAN
CHANGE THE WORLD

It is when we find ourselves rather than others to be the strangers, that we may find ourselves living in the real American world almost as if for the first time. It's embarrassing to say, but in walking down streets of Brooklyn for a couple of hours as the only white person I could see, I became belatedly aware that white is a color. I realized I was colored, just like everyone else in the world. My color was white. I kept walking. I made it to the appointed street for my afternoon engagement.

Throughout the hot afternoon, I sat with two other volunteers on rugs we had thrown out on the sidewalk in front of a row of tenements, and read library books to children and helped them paint pictures of their neighborhood. I was constantly aware of being watched now by two older black men: one sitting in, the other standing next to, an abandoned car parked in an alleyway three doors down. A grandmother sat on a stoop, two teens shot hoops at a basketball rim on a pole, cars drove by as a young girl watched from an upstairs window. Seeing through color- blind eyes is one thing; the desire to *be seen* through color-blind eyes is quite another. But as we were saying our goodbyes to the kids, one of the men in the alley went out of his way, subtly, to catch my eye. It didn't take him long. When he had it, he nodded to me, as if to let me know that if this was what I was here to do, I was welcome on his street anytime.

It was one brief and blessed moment of color blindness between two Americans, a moment filled with the promise of changes in heart, in a land of both fulfilled, and unfulfilled, promises.

26

GIVING RULE-BREAKING THE BENEFIT OF THE DOUBT

"Why do you spend your money for that which is not bread, and your labor for that which does not satisfy? Listen diligently to me, and eat what is good, and delight yourselves in rich food."

—Isaiah 55:2 (English Standard Version)

Listening with our mouth full is never considered impolite. All Jesus ever said about receiving hospitality was to take and eat what is set before us, with whomever we find ourselves. I have a friend who helps serve up three or four hot meals a week in a city that includes all weights and sizes, classes and professions. He says, "We invite everyone and anyone to come eat our meals. If they're poor, they need to eat. If they're rich, they need to eat with the poor." The terms *rich* and *poor* are obviously relative (sometimes relatives!), and it's a good exercise to try to think of a meal in our life when we were likely the richest person at the table, and another occasion when we were likely the poorest.

I remember sharing more than one meal in New Jersey with a German particle physicist named Oola, who was far richer in education and worldly experience than I was. But I was in seminary at the time and he was an atheist, so I thought of myself vainly as a bit richer in spirituality than he was. He professed to dislike Christians who smiled too much, but he came over from his university to our seminary once a week or so, as he said, "to eat the salad bar with Jesus." He cooked for us once in western Nebraska, on his way across the country in a $200 car ("I talked them down to $195," he said proudly). He was wending his way west around the world through Los Angeles and Hong Kong on a counterintuitive path to a new London teaching gig. He said what he was cooking for us that evening didn't have enough fat. "Do you have any lard?" he asked. I knew I should be appalled. But I also knew my Bible, and ate everything Oola put on my plate. It was delicious.

27

EVERY STORY HAS A
LIFE OF ITS OWN

Every story told can lead to larger ones, if it's allowed to just spin itself out. At the church preschool where I served for five years in Point Loma, California, I did twenty-minute chapels for the three- to five- year-olds once a month. Mainly I just told them a story with a few props and a prayer. We hoped they'd remember something from it all one day.

I told the story of Zacchaeus one month, the short, unpopular tax collector who stood in a tree one day to see Jesus over the crowd. I chose a nice, floppy, three-foot African American doll from the prop room (diversity is good, even among dolls), a fireplace poker to give him a spine, and a rope to keep him tethered. I went out to hide Zacchaeus up in a small leafed-out ash tree outside the chapel, to hopefully stay up there until I could call to him and point him out to the children later. But just as I stepped out of the church, a large moving van pulled up next to the curb, and along with the driver, two "day loaders" stepped out onto the sidewalk in front of the church, from their homes in central LA. They were both black, and before I could get my foot off the ground into the tree, one said as clear as day, stopped dead cold serious in his tracks, "You're not going to hang that doll in that tree."

I looked at him, startled, and then down at myself and saw that I was suddenly a white man in a white neighborhood holding a black doll and a rope in my hands, getting ready to climb a tree. I said without hesitation, "No, I'm not. I'm going to get a different doll." I stepped out from the shade, gently pushed his shoulder and told him I heard him, but also who Zacchaeus was and what this tax collector before him was actually going to climb up into that tree to do. Forty-five minutes later as kids were settling in, with a pale Zacchaeus watching us quietly from above, the young black man caught my eye as he was climbing back into the semi's cab to leave, and lifted his chin.

"I think I remember that story from Sunday school," he said.

IF JESUS IS NOT REAL, HE
IS NO ONE AT ALL

The pursuit of constant, perfect happiness can make one very unhappy. It's not only unnecessary, but it's also not what Jesus himself was after. Now that I'm no longer a professional Christian (I mean I'm no longer a pastor), I've gained the freedom to take a different kind of look at Jesus. He can, of course, bear and survive any look one wants to give him. I've been reminded he can look different from the back pews than he does every Sunday morning from the pulpit. I now like to imagine him sitting across a pub or a restaurant from me, at a far corner table having a leisurely afternoon glass of wine or even whiskey with friends or strangers both—he seems comfortable enough either way. I try to imagine what he might be saying, without me making it up for him. Most of the time now, I see him mostly listening.

When the pub is full, I've been learning to pretend I don't know who the man in the corner is, or to at least not wear my familiarity with his story too quickly on my sleeve. I think it's making me a better listener myself. When I catch myself trying to fix people's unhappiness with easy-peasy Jesus answers, I glance back across the room at the man himself, pause, and start thinking again. The storied Jesus seems to me no doubt a man full of presence without being full of easy answers— full of joy without always being happy. He cried in sorrow over the loss of friends, he complained about being abandoned, he prayed at times that his experience would be anything but what it was. Sometimes I wonder if his real gift was in never letting a false smile cross his face, nor a false note cross his lips. He didn't wish anyone unhappy trails, but he liked to be with people where they were, not where they smiled and wished or imagined themselves to be.

Jesus may have been real good, but never without being good and real.

IF CHARITY BEGINS AT HOME,
WHERE DOES IT END?

The question about belonging is a question about the boundaries around whom we consider worthy of love and care. Just who is family, anyway? From the moment I got the text, there was no question I was going. She was family, and I had loved her since she was in a crib. But would I do what I was about to do if she were a total stranger? The text came mid-evening, and ten minutes later I was dressed and out the door. There was no question I was going.

My beloved niece Anna had rolled her pickup three times on a Colorado freeway exit nearby, and she was in an emergency hospital bed a mile from our home with a concussion, two broken ribs, a broken neck, and lacerations to the body. There was no question I was going. You know what you would do. Over the next forty-eight hours, there were kisses on the forehead, quiet talks with doctors and nurses, phone calls with towing companies, hotel clerks, and insurance adjusters—all extended with as much kindness, courtesy, and doggedness as possible. There was never any question I was going to help. She's family. But I did find myself two days later, as I carried a pillow and a pair of ski boots across an auto salvage lot, wondering whether I could feel just as natural in the act of helping someone if they were a complete stranger to me.

30

BUILDING COMMUNITY IS THE
REAL PURPOSE OF CHARITY

If the aim of our charitable giving is off a bit, maybe we need to adjust our target. At the end of *Annie Hall*, Woody Allen's Oscar-winning Best Picture, he comments on the crazy value of stepping into relationships time after time even after they've gone bad and one's been deeply hurt—by telling an old joke. A man goes to the psychiatrist and says, "Our brother's crazy; he thinks he's a chicken." The doctor asks why the man doesn't turn in his brother. The man then says, "We would, except that . . . we need the eggs."

Somehow the egg (the soul) of the family's brother was more valuable than his craziness, or their own for that matter. When the Bible invites its readers to "think of ways to motivate one another to acts of love and good works," it calls forth vulnerability in the face of painfully crazy problems with no easy solutions. Vulnerable can feel crazy. "I tried helping someone once and I got burned," we say. Or we say, "There's no guarantee anything I do is going to make a bit of difference to anyone's problems anyway."

But what if permanently fixing problems isn't the ultimate point and aim of true charity? What if the problems themselves we will always have with us, but it's the souls *with* problems that are the point and aim of true love? Just as we were all as children, once upon a time, welcomed as vulnerable newborns, with charity, into a family or community larger than ourselves, maybe we all know deep down the cherished gifts in life that become available over time to any soul that discovers it belongs.

Crazy as solving problems can seem at times, maybe it's never just about feeding the chickens or counting their problems. It's always about gathering, and cherishing, the eggs (the souls) themselves.

31

COMPELLED BY TRUE LOVE

When we find ourselves having chosen whom to love, can we really choose what happens next? Hurricane Michael hit Florida's Panhandle one recent early October, and in the aftermath of widespread mandatory evacuation orders, I was struck by headlines that said someone or some family was "forced to stay." So what is it that might force someone to stay put in the face of their own physical demise?

On an MSNBC news show the afternoon of the landfall, the host interviewed by phone a woman in a coastal town twenty-six feet above sea level. The woman said she lived paycheck to paycheck and was forced to stay because none of the shelters in her county were set up to take pets. Obviously she wasn't forced by anyone to stay in her home. She was "forced" by love of another creature. The news report strangely comforted me. I did not judge her for loving.

My thought was that truly charitable community holds itself together by intentionally taking this same kind of risky love for other creatures. When human strangers we do not personally know are in danger of being swamped by forces beyond their control, we hear of it over the wires and it gets our attention. We know that care has to be made available for them from someone, somewhere, in the midst of their trouble—even if it is not our trouble. The news of other human troubles stops us in our tracks and we ponder, at least for a moment. We stay home with these strangers in our imaginations, waiting out the storm with them, sharing our ample supplies of thoughts and prayers. And sometimes we share even more.

All because on some level we fellow human beings discover, like the woman on the news, that we just have to.

32

THE WILLINGNESS TO SEE IS
A GIFT IN AND OF ITSELF

It is what we start seeing after we've seen it all that counts the most. Henry David Thoreau spent his entire life within the region of his native town, Concord, Massachusetts, but he saw more there, all around him, than most. "I have travelled a great deal in Concord," he wrote, and he regarded it as a kindness that his lack of wealth had nailed him down to one region for so long, and had made him study and love that one spot of earth more and more. As a young man, Thoreau once climbed a white pine tree to its very top, and saw mountains in the distance he had never seen before. But the best thing he discovered was at the very tops of the trees themselves: "a few minute and delicate red cone-like blossoms, the fertile flower of the white pine . . . [expanded] only toward the heavens, above men's heads and unobserved by them." Thoreau carried one of these blossoms into the town square and showed it around to choppers and farmers and hunters, "and not one had ever seen the like before, but they wondered as at a star dropped down."

Not seeing is learned too. Learning to see again, as if for the first time, can require acts of patience and deliberate will, especially if what we're looking for is what is true and real but not necessarily pleasant to see. We may be surprised by what treasures we find when we're motivated simply out of a sense of curiosity—about what's at the top of the next tree, over the next mountain, or around the next corner. All Thoreau seems to have done is have the courage to open his sense of wonder and let himself wander, and then share with others what he saw. Could the beginnings of charity in our own hearts simply be a measure of the same courage? What about climbing into the village woods where we live with a sense of compassion and respect, letting ourselves see unflinchingly who is there beneath us, above us, around us, and beyond, and then sharing who and what we discover with the world?

This gift, too, is not only about remunerations to the soul of the one who sees, but also of the one who is seen. Being noticed and acknowledged is one of the most life-changing and inspiring experiences anyone can have in this world— especially for those who have never experienced it before.

33

WE ARE SURROUNDED WHEREVER WE ARE BY PEOPLE WORTHY OF OUR ATTENTION

"You can observe a lot by watching," Yogi Berra once famously observed. Henry David Thoreau's essay called "Walking" was published in *The Atlantic* in 1862. "The walking of which I speak," he wrote, "has nothing in it akin to taking exercise ... as the Swinging of dumb-bells or chairs; but is itself the enterprise and adventure of the day. If you would get exercise, go in search of the springs of life." Thoreau thought of taking walks as an art form, more like sauntering than merely getting somewhere on foot; his kind was best done like a camel, he said, "the only beast which ruminates when walking." Who knows what soulful treasures await us when we wander in pure wonder on nothing but our whims!

The word *saunter*, Thoreau tells his readers, is beautifully derived "'from idle people who roved about the country in the Middle Ages, asking charity under pretense of going *a la Sainte Terre*,' to the Holy Land, till the children exclaimed, 'There goes a *Sainte-Terrer*,' a Saunterer, a Holy-Lander."

Where exactly are the holy lands, anyway? Could they be closer to our own homes and towns than we think? I find myself wondering if the simple act of walking with friends through both strange and familiar neighborhoods, with intentionally focused and charitable eyes, might not promise to make us all Saunterers too.

SEEING BEAUTY IN THE MIDST OF THE MUNDANE

Seeing the world around us begins right where we believe we've already sensed all there is to see. "Mostly all we need to do is look and listen, touch and taste," as the author, Bible translator, and Montana native Eugene Peterson tells it. Peterson was talking about noticing value and beauty already around us by describing a decision he and his wife had made to become bird-watchers. Birds were all around them, and they decided to be oblivious to them no longer. A young friend, an accomplished bird-watcher, helped them get started, and together they drove south along Flathead Lake, a marshy area just south of Elmo, Montana. Elmo, as Peterson knew it well, was a very small town in a poor, depressed place. There is really nothing there, he said, "just a few flimsy houses, each with a rusted-out 1951 Ford disintegrating in the front yard and a doorless refrigerator on the porch." After they had passed through the town, their friend David asked them how many different birds they had seen. Peterson and his wife hadn't seen any.

"I counted nine species," said David.

CHARITY IN THE LAND
OF THE FREED

"Our soul is escaped as a bird out of the snare of the fowlers: The snare is broken, and we are escaped." Psalm 124:7 (American Standard Version)

Once we are freed from our need to be loved in return, we are freed to give. Andrea was behind bars for years once upon a time, but she's uncageable now. She will tell you with a huge smile on her face about the day she was freed while still in prison. It was her lowest day, and also her highest. She came to herself after years in trouble on the streets, by coming face-to-face with a presence in the world beyond herself. Now you can't wipe that smile off her face (at least while I'm looking!). You also cannot keep her from packing up hygiene kits and sandwiches and fried chicken dinners and shoes and socks and jackets every Monday morning and delivering them to homeless people she has met who are still on the streets, each fighting their own personal battles with traumatic family and other background experiences. Sometimes others join her in these missions; sometimes she goes alone. Sometimes others help with the expenses; sometimes she just pays for it all herself.

I suggested once that we write a year's worth of weekly stories about these struggling street people by name, and two days later she had written down twenty-three names of local people she already knew and had a relationship with. If it is possible to be completely street-savvy and fearless at the same time, that fits Andrea to a T. The depth of her compassion for those who have been left behind seems fathomless. She's been to the same bottom they are on, and now she does not seem able to remember who she is without remembering who they are too. She is co-designer and manager of our Wildbird Treasure Nest Boutique in Washington, but her real work is as a fireball of inspiration to us all, and all who meet her.

We listen to more than what she says. All we mainly do around her is watch and learn from what she does and who she is, as we wonder with awe at how free and unencumbered her soul is now as she does it.

WHERE TRUE TREASURE
LIES HIDDEN

Giving the gift of connection is never wasted for the giver.

Urban prospectors still pan for gold in downtown Denver, often near Confluence Park west of Coors Field where Cherry Creek flows into the South Platte River. You can watch the modern amateur prospectors from time to time from a deck above, outside REI/Starbucks, as they labor with their hands in the water and their heads down in the sun beneath the city skyline still rising beyond. Experience is always what you get when you don't get what you want, and these recreational seekers after gold flakes are getting rich in experience! They sift down repeatedly into the sand and gravel for the ancient treasure that promises to lift us all up.

Eight or nine blocks south of this park, my wife and I checked into a hotel one Christmas Eve years ago, to take in the city's carolling atmosphere and a symphony-enhanced service in a vaulted ceiling church sanctuary, all with the season's treasure of an experience of "community" on our hearts and minds. Mid-afternoon temperatures were in the teens, and unless you were hunting for ice crystals, prospecting season was over. Family was not with us, all our friends were with family. What was left to us was the city, and we took it in like a lost relative. In the morning the streets were subfreezing, quiet and empty, except for a series of steel grates lining the sidewalks, steam rising above each one from below the streets, with a homeless man or woman lying prostrate on almost every one of them. On our way to our car, we looked down on the grate man just outside the back of our hotel in wonder, like prospectors gazing into a stream.

We snagged a banana and a warm muffin off a neighboring hotel's breakfast bar and tucked them near his blanketless body with a five-dollar bill. Without lifting his head, he opened his eyes, gathered our gifts close to his chest, and mumbled to us, clear as day, "Merry Christmas." We didn't say it to him; he said it to us.

We're not sure it was a moment for him, but it was a moment for us. In our search for treasures of human connection, not all that is gold glitters.

37

COURAGE IS A GIFT
ANYONE CAN GIVE

The gift of courage can simply mean refusing to give up. Willard was the poorest man I have ever known personally. He was one of the most vulnerable, yet also one of the most spiritually resilient. The presence of grace and truth came to Willard through other people, just as it also came to them through him. "I shook Mother Teresa's hand one day," Willard tells me. Seriously, I respond.

"I was in the Oakland county jail, and Mother Teresa came to visit, insisting that she shake the hand of every inmate in the prison before she left." Willard had now been sober for more than a dozen years, ever since he met his wife one evening at a soup kitchen, and she'd insisted that he be dry if they had any future. They were now raising two grandchildren in their month-to-month, rented, transitory home, from which they moved on sometimes more than twice a year.

"I met Miss America at our soup kitchen once," he told me one afternoon. Seriously, I respond. "She was only Miss Nebraska then, but I told her I knew I was meeting the next Miss America." Willard was right. I asked him to speak one time at a regional church gathering, remembering to this day only one thing Willard said in his low, slow and measured cadence. "I've supported soup kitchens for many years," he told us all. "Soup kitchens are important, because, you know . . . you're hungry."

38

ALONG WITH INDIVIDUALS, COMMUNITIES THEMSELVES CAN STAND FOR SOME CORRECTION

In one moment a light can dawn and reveal another soul's entire life struggle. Willard had never been to war, but you could smell the smoke of another kind of battle on his skin. Trauma comes in many shapes and sizes, and Willard's was no secret from the world. He was Lakota. His life had not been my life, but I was honored that we could for a season simply call each other friend. The battles that came for him had come early, when he was relocated as a child by the federal government from his native lands in South Dakota to the concrete backstreets of Oakland, California. A government initiative to give his family some different clothes, a different language, and a different cultural start would mean Native American families like his would be made over from scratch to become, well, American. He'd given up early and had spent decades on skid row in the Bay Area and in Denver. Yet he had never given up. Adults can bring traumas onto themselves, but children do not. Trauma comes to them sometimes with the territory, sometimes with the tribe.

I went on a mission retreat with Willard into the Black Hills when he was in his early sixties, and we shared a canoe at twilight before dinner. Fish jumped and a beaver splashed. As we pulled onto shore, he said quietly, "That was fun."

Then after a pause, he added, "I've never been in a canoe before."

39

LISTENING REVEALS WHAT CANNOT BE SEEN

Calling struggling strangers by their name is one of the most radical acts of charity in this world. Poor people all have a name, and it's not "the poor." I stood once years ago in a deluge of rain with half a dozen others while we handed a young mother a bag of fresh groceries, and she gave us her name. Denisa, she said. An act of hospitality on both sides.

She stood just inside the blanket-draped doorway of a cinder block migrants' hovel in Baja Mexico, not far from a farm field full of flowers. Two young barefoot sons looked up with eager faces beside her. A hot plate balanced on a chair behind them; a single electric light bulb hung from a rafter in the corner. Water dripped through the roof onto the concrete floor. We were a religious group and said we wanted to say a prayer for her family, and we asked what she would like prayers for. I knew for sure what she was going to say. It was obvious to us all that she needed food and a roof more than anything else. But instead she swept her tearing and tired eyes across our faces, as if to see if we were serious, as she said, "My marriage."

Denisa gave the real gift that day. She told us she was just like us, and she gave us her name.

HELPING OUR NEIGHBORS
COME ALL THE WAY HOME

A relationship of trust is always the first step. Charity gets short-changed in the popular imagination, by people thinking it automatically has more to do with opening our pocketbooks than with simply opening our eyes and ears and hearts. So many of us need guides to show us what we do not see, to help us listen to voices we may not immediately recognize. With the steady leadership of people like Harry, people can learn to see the lingering personal war wounds that were not left behind on our nation's battlefields—lingering wounds suffered by veterans of inner wars that have never stopped. We all need reminders that these wounds came home with them, and remain so often hidden in plain sight all around us. We are inspired by Harry's devotion, and that of other men and women like him. He will fearlessly go anywhere and talk to anyone. When I ask him if he's ever afraid walking up to a solitary vet's trailer or home in the woods, he says, "Well, if they don't shoot you, you're fine!" He's been there, done that, suffered there, seen that. He starts with a cup of coffee and a listening ear. Can that ever be enough?

Yes, a start is always an abundance when compared to not starting. A "Hello, my name is Harry" to a man living alone in the woods is always an abundance when compared to neglectful avoidance. A "What can be done?" or a "How can I help?" is always an abundance when compared to the certainty of helplessness, even if one discovers there's not much else one can offer at the moment. Wildbird as an organized charity isn't always sure what it can do to help solve individual veterans' problems in the big picture. But it is learning from people like Harry that solving veterans' problems isn't always the answer, that it's the people with the problems who matter. And there are always ways any community can help return the wounded home again. Even if it starts with just names, a handshake, and a lousy cup of coffee.

41

WE ARE BIGGER THAN OUR WOUNDS, EVEN THOUGH SCARS REMAIN

To the mind and body of a soldier who has seen war, the battles are never completely over. My mom's father was in his early twenties when the Great War came for him. In the autumn of 1918, he found his hands holding a rifle in a field in France, having spent most of his formative years with his hands holding a plow in a field in Minnesota. Advancing one evening with his platoon through mud fields and barbed wire, Private Harry was shot through the neck and upper arm, and he dove into a foxhole with a fellow soldier. He remained there under fire throughout that night and all the next day, until he was able to retreat back through the wire in the dark the second night to his lines. All the while, the other soldier's body lay next to him, dead from his wounds.

Harry survived and came back to marry and farm, only to lose his farm in the early stages of the Great Depression. He moved his family to the Twin Cities, where he delivered milk and worked maintenance for a dairy company until he retired. He never regained the nerve to buy a house in all his years in the city. He quietly raised a small family and a huge garden, hunted and fished and pulled through. He was tough as nails when it came to physical pain, and he kept his head down and his spirits up the best he could. Wounds can heal, but their scars remain. The internal scars were always there for his grandchildren to see, as visible as the scars on his neck and arm, which he would show them anytime they asked.

He had passed wounded as an adult through the war and the depression decades before, but neither one of those wounds stopped him from living and giving throughout the rest of his long life.

OLD SOLDIERS CARRY THEIR PERSONAL BATTLES IN PEACETIME LIKE THEY ONCE CARRIED THEIR COUNTRY'S BATTLES IN WAR

Circumstances of war do not make a man; they reveal him. Howard grew up poor on a Kansas farm, until World War II came for him. He served in the United States Marine Corps, driving and training and maintaining heavy equipment, including tanks. He served and was wounded on Iwo Jima, and stayed in for a decade after the Second World War, just long enough to find himself on (and sometimes behind) battle lines again in the U.S. Marines' decisive Battle of Chosin Reservoir in Korea. Driving huge wreckers on the Korean Peninsula, Howard was asked to make his way under cover of darkness many nights beyond enemy lines in order to retrieve valuable American equipment that had been disabled but not destroyed.

When the marines retreated in the face of large Chinese forces, Howard came back from one late mission, among the last marines to evacuate. With two large pieces of equipment in his charge, the only ship that had not yet left port was under the command of a Japanese officer, who told Howard that there was no more room. Howard and his fellow marine, neither of them officers, pulled their pistols and told the officer to make room. He made room, Howard said. Then he added, "We never told him we had run out of ammunition two days earlier."

In his mid-nineties now, Howard still watches and listens to distant fireworks with family on July 4, but he grows very quiet. He raised a family and volunteered his experience and resources for years on behalf of the Boy Scouts and orphanages in Baja California, and until they cut him off for reasons of his own health, Howard donated close to fifteen gallons to the local blood bank over the course of his lifetime.

Howard left the farm and these wars decades before, but the lessons they taught him never left him. The harsh realities of life in war and peace did not defeat him; instead they informed every decision he made for the rest of his life.

43

THEY ALSO SERVE WHO ONLY LAUGH AND DRIVE

Not every life story is told with words; for some the life within them is their story. For some small-town people where I grew up, a local evangelist could be just as annoying as a town drunk. But either a drunk or an evangelist is at his best when he can at least also make you laugh. Our family friend Ralph was only one of these, a natural, irrepressible evangelist, unless you count being drunk on the spirit of life. Ralph grew up poor, the son of a school custodian, and by his own admission . . . *wild*! He got drafted into the army in World War II, but he never saw a battlefield. He spent four years on a base in Florida driving an ambulance, and he never lost his love of fast cars and great stories, nor his hatred of standing in line for anything. "Lift up your chin, poke out your chest, hold a clipboard close to your ribs," he would say, "and you could go anywhere you wanted on my army base, private or no!"

He came home after the war to get a job in a hardware store, learned the plumbing trade, and smoked like a chimney until he was twenty-eight, when through an encounter with a stranger he "met Christ and got saved." My dad always said that with an education Ralph could have been a doctor or given Johnny Carson a run for his money, he was so incredibly funny. Oh, the stories Ralph could tell and double his audience over, catching their breath as they listened! And the story of the new life that had come to him was his favorite story to tell of all.

But Ralph was not a doctor or a lawyer or a preacher or a comedian. He was our plumber. And we lived our clean and convenient lives by the fruits of his labor.

THE PURSUIT OF STATUS CAN BE
A DISTRACTION FROM TRUE LIFE

The gift of charitable living is given all around us every day, without media fanfare. Ralph was a man easy to dismiss if you claimed that all piety is false or if you feared religious people who bring up the word *Christ* just a little too soon in every conversation. Many townspeople would have dismissed Ralph's talk with extreme prejudice if it weren't for one annoyingly inescapable fact: despite being so human and broken, through it all Ralph was so incomprehensibly and undeniably *full of life*. Status didn't matter to him—he never had any. When sewer mains broke, he stood waist-deep in the town's muck to do the repairs. He could leave that job and shower up, and then make himself look sharper walking out of the hospital auxiliary thrift store than lesser mortals ever could walking out of Brooks Brothers.

On his meager income, Ralph raised a family, and loved traveling to Florida beaches on vacation and eating out locally on Friday nights with friends. And did I mention that as worldly as he was, he liked to pass out religious tracts and talk about his faith? He was hard to be around if you wanted to keep vulnerabilities like that private, but he was also hard to dismiss, even from the other side of the street. Widowed and living on medical disability in his later years, he finally succumbed to a heart attack late one night, hammering away alone against the rafters in his own small basement, trying to earn a few extra dollars a month by renting out a room or two.

When I heard the news, a small piece of ground gave way beneath my feet. I knew our fair city had just lost one of the very richest men in town.

45

SERIOUS GIVING DOES NOT
HAVE TO BE DONE SOMBERLY

Respectful levity is sometimes the last thing we think of when offering help to those in dire straits. I didn't meet Danny until the following morning, but he'd definitely been there with us in spirit the night before. Wildbird had hosted a gathering for twenty-five people at a hotel in Bellingham, Washington, where among friends and strangers we'd passed around some appetizers and wine, some stories, and a handheld wireless microphone. We'd listened as volunteers told about Wildbird initiatives among struggling schoolchildren, homeless families, and veterans. Somehow when the lights were out at the end of the night, I found myself in possession of two cardboard to-go boxes full of more cheese and crackers than I could ever healthily devour myself.

So I stopped my SUV at a rainy intersection the next morning, where a single man in his late twenties stood without a sign, a large black tarp covering his possessions. When he came to the window, he told me his name was Danny and called me sir, and I told him I had a wine and cheese party for him and his friends—without the wine! He took the boxes and said that would be a new one, a homeless man throwing a wine and cheese party in the park! I wished him well and drove away, figuring it was only fitting that Danny and his friends should share in a bit of our fun, as well as receiving a bit of our help.

46

TRUTH BE TOLD

Truth be told, all of humanity is connected by the wound of being human. The other day I was stopped in my tracks by two men downtown in Colorado. One of these men's crippled, contorted body stood squarely in front of me, holding a cardboard sign, just as the other man's voice started ringing in my ears. I averted my eyes from Jess at first because I doubted, as usual, that everything written on his sign was factually true. It said he was a vet with cancer who needed help getting to Las Vegas for a job. The only part of the sign undeniably true was the cancer: it was written all over his face. His jaw was half-gone, and three different colors of puffy skin had been grafted over his surgical wounds.

I walked ten yards before the YouTube voice of the other man, that modern-day theo-economic prophet of our time, Walter Brueggemann, started whispering to me, telling me to turn around and put my money where my charitably talkative mouth was. I walked back and said hello, and found that Jess could barely utter a word; he had to trace his name for me in the air. When I stood close to hear and looked directly into his face, the truthfulness of his sign no longer mattered. He was obviously a veteran of many kinds of battle, and job or no job in Vegas, here he was still trying, his life not over, a visual pariah who I imagined had social troubles even among his fellow homeless on the streets. When I handed him a twenty to help him on his way, he shook my hand firmly and thanked me with his eyes. I didn't care in that moment if his entire sign was nothing but fake news; I had told him a twenty was all I had to give him, which wasn't exactly true either. There was a much larger human story going on here, and it haunted me.

When I drove back two hours later to find him, to give him another twenty and ask him for his story, all that was left where he had stood was his sign. I wandered and waited in vain for an hour, and then leaned his cardboard story over to protect the marker ink from the coming rain—a rain that was just beginning to fall.

NO ONE RETIRES FROM THEIR NEED FOR COMMUNITY

It is not only those who give the gift who give the gift. Priscilla is ninety-three and lives alone now in her home in Seattle, except that her son and daughter take turns staying with her to help her as they can. People who know how sharp she is call her "a real pistol." She used to be the person in her church's ladies guild who for years ran a tight ship in the parish's large kitchen—she and she alone was in charge of the chicken! Now she has at least one meal delivered to her every week by another group of women, thirty years younger, who have simply decided to give back to seniors like Priscilla. One of these younger women taking this small but meaningful initiative is Deb, a longtime corporate executive who is now a real estate broker in the greater Seattle area, who shares with her team a commitment to experimenting with charitable living—helping others know they belong.

Theirs is a small operation where the cooking is done in the younger women's own kitchens, but to Priscilla what they deliver is more than a meal. She looks forward not only to the food they bring but also to the visit that comes with it. One time she was so excited about their coming that she put on a fresh dress and makeup and tied two pink bows in her hair to greet them at the door.

48

WEARING OUR HEARTS ON OUR SLEEVE IS A GOOD START TO WEARING THEM ON OUR FEET

Sometimes the people who say they have no personal dreams to pursue are the very ones who like to make others' dreams come true. Our friend Phill is one of these people. People who know Phill well don't believe him about the "no dreams" part, but about the making-dreams-happen part, this description is hard to argue with.

Phill is one of the hardest workers I know, in charity or business, who still wears his heart on his sleeve. When telling a story about an encounter with a struggling family or a hungry schoolchild or a teenager falling through the cracks of a major-city mainline school system, Phill is always the first one whose eyes tear up. Phill has then learned to put his feet where his heart is.

After growing up in Salem, Oregon, around construction and agriculture in his youth (he used to hoe mint fields during his high school summers, where everyone wore winter coats all day despite the heat because the cooling effect of mint on one's skin is the same as on one's mouth), Phill raised his family just across the Canadian border in Vancouver, British Columbia. After his university degree was finished, Phill co-founded an alternative high school for kids who were falling through the cracks in the regular districts, and he served as principal of that school for thirty-seven years. He's taken those students (and his family) traveling coast to coast and border to border and beyond, hiking and camping along continental wilderness trails, and on cultural excursions within their own city and abroad. Phill has traveled with his family halfway around the world on yearlong mission trips.

Phill is a real estate broker now, but he also works on and cajoles his community into charitable pursuits. He's hard not to want to work with. Backpack weekend food programs for schoolchildren in several local districts are his main passion these days. But even one man's brief initiatives can come to have a life of their own. Last year he spearheaded a community drive to bring Christmas baskets full of food resources and toys to fifteen different families in his local area, each worth about $500. When his own time and energy resources were not sufficient to effectively repeat the gift the second year, two of his volunteers from the first year undertook six Christmas baskets of their own in a nearby impoverished neighborhood. They had been reminded with us all that wearing our hearts on our sleeves isn't all that far from learning to wear them on our feet.

49

THE MUSIC IS STILL REAL EVEN WHEN IT'S NOT YET IN PERFECT TUNE

The spiritual power of helping others experience being seen can come at a cost to the ones who see. The professional term used to describe the gift of seeing someone else's suffering, whether that suffering is *fixable* or not, is what the German author Alice Miller called being an "enlightened witness."

Serving in a rural mental health center in the American West for several years, Sally worked as a clinical psychologist—a professional enlightened witness—among an underserved, traumatized, often hidden American population. The stories she heard and the lives she encountered opened her eyes to realities she could never again unsee in the world all around her. Sometimes she could do someone some good; sometimes a day in the therapeutic trenches simply broke her heart. One of Sally's psychotic clients once tagged his own horrendous childhood abuse story as "'you know, the horrification." A respected and seasoned colleague who worked as a home liaison came into staffing one day with a stunned horror in her own eyes and said, "You wouldn't believe what I saw in a hoarder's house this morning. I can't stay today; I've got to go home."

Two weeks later, Sally sat in the back pew of a church and listened to the most beautiful duet being sung. She could only sit and weep, as one of the two singing was this very colleague. Sometimes there's nothing to do with tears but to cry them, as we keep singing the song.

CHARITABLE LIVING IS NOT MEANT TO BE ONLY IN OUR DREAMS

Forgotten languages still have meaning for those who listen.

On an almost daily basis, my wife and I share with one another over morning coffee whatever dream, or even mere snippets of dreams, we happen to remember from the night before. Sally shared one morning a snippet she said was all she could remember from a much longer, epic dream—a dream in which she observed a dime slightly buried in some leaves and dirt beside a bus stop bench.

In *Dreams: God's Forgotten Language*, the Jungian analyst and Episcopalian priest John A. Sanford wrote that "as events that take place in our world, [dreams] have as much right to careful study as any other event in nature. So far we haven't found anything in nature that doesn't have its function. So why should we say that of all created things the dream alone makes no sence?" But what sense can be made of such a dream as Sally's? Like everything else in life, the first choice is whether or not to listen more closely.

She continued: "As I reached down to pick the dime up, I then saw a nickel, which I also plucked from the dirt. Then a quarter, a bit more buried under the leaves, twigs, and dirt—a lot of quarters. I realized that various people had made donations to this slightly hidden cache, so that people who didn't have the fare could still take the bus. I put the coins I had picked up back into the dirt, and made note of this act of communal generosity to another person walking by. I said, 'It looks like there are several dollars in there.' The passerby found it important to tell me there was in fact ten dollars in coins being stored under there, hidden away for some stranger's rainy day."

That was it. What sense would you make of that dream if it were yours? I told my wife that I didn't know what it meant, but that I liked it. It made me feel as though there is more abundance beneath the dirt and leaves of our daily lives than is readily visible on the surface.

Kind of like the abundance of meaning that lies hidden within our dreams.

EVERY STORY IS ABOUT
MORE THAN ITSELF

When in doubt, check it out—tell the story one more time.
In the coastal city of Charleston, South Carolina, I worked nearly every day for seven years at telling stories of the city's history to others like me, who weren't from there. The job was to tell the story of the city, but there were always more facets of that story than one could tell in one sitting, or in one walking, or on one leisurely harbor cruise. If you let your curiosity run, it was a story of which you could trace the beginnings, but to which you could never find the end. There were wars and hurricanes, earthquakes and fires, wealth and slavery, gardens and churches and Caribbean architecture, human heroics and heartbreaking betrayals. And if you didn't tell it quite right, in another couple of hours you'd get another chance to tell it just a little differently, to new strangers to whom it was all as fresh as a blossoming crepe myrtle tree in the spring. And because it was fresh to them, it could turn fresh for you, too, again and again and again.

From the wealthiest city per capita in the United States before the Civil War to one of the poorest for a century after, those hundred years of abject poverty and political debasement had served to save the city's homes and buildings from destruction; no one could afford to tear down their homes and build new ones. And now the old houses were being protected (and bought and sold) like gold. How could you not tell a story like that every day, in every which way, and not find the story of yourself and your own family and all of humanity in it? I no longer ask for whom any story's told; it's always told for me.

52

HOME IS BOTH A LANDING PAD FOR THE JOURNEY BEHIND, AND A LAUNCHING PAD FOR THE JOURNEY AHEAD

Just when we think we've pretty much arrived at this spiritual love thing, we discover we have only just begun. In mid-life (at least I hope it was mid-life!), I dropped myself into one seminary in the east and two pulpits in the west, and found myself saying, almost in apology, that I was a writer trying really hard to become a preacher. Twenty years later, the flow of that river is reversing upstream again. My earlier sermons are almost unreadable to me now—not because of what they say but because of what they don't say. They're like guardrails of theological caution along the shoulders of a road of faith, but theology is not faith—at its best the former flows uneasily from the latter. My theology is still in fine form, and I love talking the talk with anyone with a similar love. But as those fervent Irish Christian U2 guys sing, "I still haven't found what I'm looking for."

My own new frontier is an inquiry into the *experience* of a life with faith or belief or charity or grace or Jesus or whatever someone wants to call it—the real experience without all the sharp ambiguous edges trimmed off. Experience isn't always pretty, but if it's honored in our search for truth, I've become amazed at how trustworthy it can be. I wonder if I'm now glimpsing experiential shadows on the path of the ancient saints, as alongside that great and fervent North African Christian, St. Augustine, who asked himself long after his conversion and confessions, "What do I love when I love my God?" My own confession of experience these days is more modern and less high-minded, more in line with that famous Jewish American Christian of our own changing times, Bob Dylan, when he sings that after all this time he's still "just trying to get to heaven before they close the door."

HOME FREE

THE GIFT OF
THE EXTRA MILE

The Real Work

It may be that when we no longer know what to do we have come to our real work, and that when we no longer know which way to go we have come to our real journey. The mind that is not baffled is not employed. The impeded stream is the one that sings.

—Wendell Berry

If we're on the road home together, aren't we halfway home already? Princeton Theological Seminary has long had a commitment to extending its educational resources across the globe, through access to its library and its on-campus academic offerings. In this pursuit it welcomes many international students from countries around the world each year, mostly for postgraduate studies in theology after the students have already earned pastoral degrees at seminaries in their own native countries.

Out of sheer curiosity at first, I volunteered my services to help orient these students at the beginning of each year, they often being the academic cream of the crop from their respective cultures. Later, I realized, I had volunteered for my own education. I mean, why travel necessarily to Vietnam, China, Germany, Mexico, Cameroon, India, or Australia to learn from the natives of those countries, when their natives have already come to you? I also realized quickly that foreigners of all stripes have their own challenges of cross-cultural courage, even after having traveled so far already.

When asked to give them one piece of advice for their year in America, I gave them the 5,000 Mile/50 Yard Rule. You're in your lonely dorm room after dark on a winter Saturday night, and you see there's an African American Baptist worship service being held in a few minutes in the chapel across the quad. You're not sure what that is or if you'd be comfortable, let alone welcome.

Go! Don't travel 5,000 miles for your education, and miss it by 50 yards.

If this rule were applied to life itself, I suppose it would say something like this: "Don't travel 5,000 miles on your own back road home, and miss home by a moment. Don't travel a mile more along your path to a life filled with charitable living and giving, and miss it by a single doubt, a solitary intractable judgment, a singular prejudice against the pain and uncertainty of the unknown. Even back roads we've never travelled before can lead the way home."

Abraham Lincoln knew the road less traveled is always experimental and rarely paved. In his last year in office, on his way to freeing the slaves and saving the Union, as the country faced widespread uncertainty as to whether the great American experiment could long endure, Abraham Lincoln was asked how it felt to be president. "Well," he said, as he would, "it reminds me of the fellow who had been tarred and feathered by a mob and was being run out of town on a rail. Someone yelled from the crowd, 'How does it feel?' and the man shouted back, 'Well, if it wasn't for the honor of the thing, I'd rather be walking!'"

Lincoln knew a thing or two about telling stories, in both good times and hard. Some of his stories were little stories, but none of them were small. He also knew a thing or two in his bones about the wisdom and risk that comes from traveling along any road marked by malice toward none and charity for all. He knew the individual's road toward the better angels of our nature has to be taken courageously, with the courage to begin where we are with the honest truth of who we are, and of who is in the world around us.

In the midst of our technological and communications revolution in these first decades of the twenty-first century, the writer Seth Godin says that there is no map for us to follow. "If you've got the wrong map, the right compass will get you home if you know how to use it," he writes. It's an interesting question to ask: If we ever found ourselves lost in the middle of the woods, would we rather have a map or a compass, given a choice of only one? Which one would help us most surely find our way to where we wanted to go?

The map of the great American experiment was changing under our nation's feet by the hour, but the law of charity for all was Lincoln's compass, and it saw us all through.

When my brother and I were growing up in the midst of various rural Nebraska crossroads, we worked long hot summers in the country, irrigating corn and milo and soybean fields for my father. We hauled and loaded tubes and pipe, and we serviced with oil and grease and wrenches roaring engines, pivots, and deep, silent wells. We checked muddy rows, chopped tall and sticky sunflower stalks, and shoveled a lot of dry dirt. It was hot and sweaty work, and the days grew long. As boys will, we pointed out one afternoon to our dad the thunderheads rising to the west. "Look at that rain coming," we told him. "We think maybe we should shut off the engines and go golfing— it looks like we're going to get one or even two inches tonight."

Dad quoted Scripture to us, which in our household always settled matters. "He who observes the clouds gets no plowing done," he said. He was telling us to love the clouds. Observe their beauty. Feel their promise. Just don't believe in them.

Believe in water. Believe in rain.

So back to work we would go. My own long days would be punctuated by lunch in Ollie's farm place kitchen, my little Ford tractor resting in the shade outside beneath the cottonwood trees. When we were finished, she would insist every time that I leave the table and take a nap on the floor of her far living room while she did the dishes. The window air conditioner purred and the clock ticked until I would awaken and slip quietly out the front cellar-pantry door, with Ollie snoring softly on her bed in the next room. Then as the yard gate closed behind me, the crunch of gravel, the heat, and the soft distant rustling of anxious cornstalks in the breeze would welcome my soul back into the workday, like a warm blanket of grounded place -- and promise.

One late mid-summer night a month later, on a dark and sultry evening in early August, Dad and I were standing out under the family porch near midnight, soaking into our noses and pores and cuffs the smell and drench and muddy splashes of a relentless rain, silent together in the midst of a spectacular lightning and thunder storm enveloping our small county. "All right," Dad said, "maybe you might as well go out and turn off the engines."

The three wells were twelve miles out into the dark, a mile or two each from the river. My quickened yet solemn walk to one of them, from the graveled shoulder where I had parked the Ranchero near the barbed wire ditch fence in the pounding rain, was a half mile of mud from the edge of the gravel road to the center of the field. All I could see ahead of me as I walked down the shadowed causeway of cornstalks in the blackness were two glowing red-hot manifolds protruding off the sides of the engine in the distance. All I could hear above the rain was the growing, low racing roar of that striving engine getting closer and louder. As I walked up, my heart slowed as I lowered the throttle and disengaged the clutch, and when the final switch was flipped and the engine died, the silence fell over the land like a thief in the night, and it was deafening. I was muddy to my knees and soaked with water from flesh to bone, in the middle of the universe and alone, and I almost shouted. We got three and a half inches of pure charity that night, and as I slipped and slopped my way back to the road, I allowed every drop to settle into my core. Then and there I let myself rest at last, almost as if every sweating inch of mud and falling drop of rain from above belonged to me, and me to the mud and to the rain.

———————

ABOUT THE AUTHOR

"Keep your heart with all diligence, for out of it spring all the issues of life."
—Proverbs 4:23 (New King James Version)

Brad Gustafson was born and raised in a rural, tightly knit religious Swedish farming community in south central Nebraska.

A church-related junior college opportunity 2,000 miles away just outside Vancouver, British Columbia, introduced him to a larger social, cultural and theological world, and his journey into that world has never ended.

In mid-life (he hopes it was mid-life!), Brad married a woman named Sally and then completed graduate studies at Princeton Theological Seminary in New Jersey. He subsequently pastored two beloved congregations, one in Southern California and one in Western Nebraska.

Then his heart and mind and soul got restless once again. With some old college friends he helped co-found Wildbird, a spiritual charitable venture in Washington State, and then started writing. He still believes there is always something soulfully new under the sun on the road ahead for all of us, finding a way to rise up beneath our feet to meet us exactly where we are right now, and lead us home from there.

———

Write the author at bradleygus@gmail.com
Or visit his website at www.bradleygus.com